The Coolest Pets

Rabbits, Mice, and Rats

Anne O'Daly

KidHaven
PUBLISHING

Published in 2024 by
KidHaven Publishing, an Imprint of Greenhaven Publishing, LLC
2544 Clinton St., Buffalo, NY 14224

Copyright © 2019 Brown Bear Books Ltd

Portions of this work were originally authored by Dawn Titmus and published as *Rabbits, Mice, and Rats.*
All new material this edition authored by Anne O'Daly.

Design Manager: Keith Davis
Picture Manager: Sophie Mortimer

Photo Credits:
Front Cover: Shutterstock: andregric tl, jiangdi bl., New Africa br, Rudmer Zwerver tr.
Interior: Dreamstime: Sergey Lavrentev 25b, Emilia Stasiak 27t; iStock: Argument 10, 11t, Nick Biemans 14, James Brey 9t, 12, CreativeNature_nl 15, cynoclub 3, Jannoon028 7b, kali9 13b, nickpo 23b; Naturepl: Mark Taylor 24, 25t, Photoshot: Picture Alliance 17b; Shutterstock: Africa Studio 5t, 23t, 29tl, Andrew Burgess 4b, Pitchayarat Chootai 19b, CKP1001 6r, Linn Currie 16–17, 17t, 20, Maslov Dmitry 9b, George Dolgikh 7c, Eric Isselee 29b, Eye Opener 7t, GOLFX 8, Jiang Hongyan 4–5, 5br, Hurst Photo 6l, Eric Isselee 18, 29t, Anika Kodydkva 4, Oksana Kuzmina 29tr, laurendotcom 21t, LiskaM 22, Photobac 10–11, Ava Peattie 21b, 19t, schankz 27b, Dmitry Skilkov 13t, Stanick 14–15, Emilia Stasiak 11b, Olesya Tseytlin 5bl, Rudmer Zwerver 1, 26.
Key: t=top, b=bottom, c=center, l=left, r=right

Cataloging-in-Publication Data

Names: O'Daly, Anne
Title: Rabbits, mice, and rats / Anne O'Daly.
Description: Buffalo, New York : Kidhaven Publishing, 2024. |
Series: The coolest pets| Includes index and glossary
Identifiers: ISBN 9781534545410 (pbk) | ISBN 9781534545427 (library bound) | ISBN 9781534545434 (ebook)
Subjects: LCSH: Mice-- Juvenile literature | Mice as pets--Juvenile literature | Pets--Juvenile literature | Rabbits--Juvenile literature | Rabbits as pets--Juvenile literature | Rats-- Juvenile literature | Rats as pets--Juvenile literature
Classification: LCC SF453.2 O33 2024 | DDC 636.9--dc23

Manufactured in the United States of America

CPSIA compliance information: Batch #CSKH24: For further information contact Greenhaven Publishing LLC at 1-844-317-7404.

Please visit our website, www.greenhavenpublishing.com.
For a free color catalog of all our high-quality books, call toll free 1-844-317-7404 or fax 1-844-317-7405.

Find us on

Contents

Choosing a Pet

Rabbits, rats, and mice make great pets. Although they are easy to look after, they all need care and attention.

Life Spans

Mice live for one to two years, and rats live for about two to three years. Rabbits can live for up to 10 years.

Living Together

Rabbits, rats, and mice all like company. They are happier living in a pair or as part of a group. Pets from the same litter make the best pairs. Keep two females or two males together and introduce them when they're young.

Buying a Pet

Baby rabbits should stay with their mothers until they are about six to eight weeks old. You can bring baby mice home when they are five weeks old and rats when they are six weeks old. Buy directly from a breeder or a good pet store. Check out notices for these pets at the vet.

Checklist

* Do you have the space for a rabbit hutch or a cage for a mouse or rat?
* Do you have the time to care for your pet every day?
* Do you have the time for cleaning the hutch or cage every week?
* Are you willing to keep two or more pets together?
* Can your family afford the food costs and vet bills?

Adopt a Pet

Rescue centers and shelters are full of pets that need new homes. Think about giving a pet from a rescue center a forever home. Rescue centers can also give you advice about the best way to care for your new pet.

Next Steps

Rabbits, rats, and mice are cute pets that are less demanding than some pets, but it is important to choose the right one. This book will help you to pick and care for your pet. Learn about six of the most popular types. Try your hand at making a fun zone for your pet. You will also find some fascinating facts about your furry friends!

Getting Started

Before you bring your pet home, you will need food and water bowls. You will also need bedding, some toys, and somewhere for your pet to live.

Checklist

* Hutch, cage, or tank large enough for your pet.
* Food dish and water bottle the right size for your pet.
* Bedding and nesting materials, litter and litter box.
* Toys and treats.
* Pet carrier for rabbits.
* Exercise wheel for rats and mice.

Food and Water

You will need a shallow ceramic or metal food dish. They are easy to clean and cannot be chewed. A water bottle is better than a dish. It keeps the water clean and cannot be tipped over.

Food dish

water bottle

Litter Box

Rabbits and rats can be trained to use a litter box. Put the box in the area where there are usually droppings. Make sure the litter is safe for your pet. Clean out the litter box regularly.

Housing Your Pet

You can keep rabbits outside in a hutch or playhouse. Rabbits can also be kept inside. Make a room in your home rabbit safe so you can let your pet out of its cage every day. You can keep rats and mice in wire cages or glass or plastic tanks. Make sure the tank has a tightly fitting mesh lid. Rats love to climb, and mice are escape artists!

Pet Carrier

You'll need a pet carrier to take your rabbit on car journeys or to go to the vet. Rabbits can get very stressed in a moving vehicle. A nervous rabbit loose in a moving car may distract the driver. You can put pet mice and rats in a small box with holes cut in it for air.

A Home for Your Pet

Your pet needs a safe and comfortable home. Think about the size of your pet and whether it will be living inside or outside.

Outside Rabbits

If you have to keep your rabbits outside, the hutch must be large enough for them to stand on their back legs, stretch, and hop around. A small wooden playhouse with a secure run attached is a good home for rabbits. Make sure it is secure from predators and in a shady spot. Give your pet a nesting box to sleep in, such as a small cardboard box lined with straw or hay.

Inside Rabbits

Pet rabbits can happily live indoors. Make sure all the rooms it goes into are safe for your pet. Rabbits like to chew, so put electric cords out of the way. Indoor rabbits will need a private space, too, such as a cage. It should be five times the size of the rabbit and have a solid floor, not a wire one, to protect your pet's feet.

Playtime

All pets need to play to keep them fit and healthy. Chewing toys will keep your pet busy. Mice love to climb and play on a wheel. Rabbits like boxes and tunnels. Rats love to climb ladders and ropes. Give your pet time out of its hutch or cage every day to exercise and explore.

Rat Homes

Rats need space to explore and exercise. Buy your pet the biggest cage you can. Put it on a raised surface away from drafts and heat sources, such as direct sun or radiators. Add bedding material and rat-safe litter. Provide a nesting box in the cage. A small cardboard box lined with soft paper tissues or paper towels makes a good nest.

Mice Homes

A wire cage or a 10-gallon (38 L) glass or plastic tank is a good home for your pet. Use a tightly fitting mesh lid with a tank. The openings in a cage need to be 0.25 inch (6 mm) or less to prevent your mouse escaping. Put bedding on the floor, such as hardwood shavings, and provide a nesting box with strips of soft tissue or paper towel.

Food and Water

Different animals eat different foods. Find out which food is best for your pet and how much you need to feed it.

Rabbit Food

Give your rabbit plenty of hay to munch on every day. Also feed it some good-quality rabbit pellets. The amount of pellets to feed depends on your rabbit's weight. Rabbits like fresh fruit and vegetables, such as apples, cabbage, broccoli, celery, and carrots. They also love dandelion leaves. Give your pet fresh water every day. Rabbits can drink out of a dish, but a water bottle keeps the water clean. Check the bottle daily to make sure it is working.

Food for Rats

Feed your pet rat good-quality rodent pellets every day. Also give it well-washed fresh fruits and vegetables, such as small pieces of watermelon, banana, kale, and dandelion leaves. Make sure your pet has fresh water in its bottle every day.

Healthy Treats

There are lots of healthy treats that rats and mice like to eat. Low-fat, low-sugar cookies, breakfast cereal, whole-wheat bread, cooked pasta, and even pizza crust can be tasty treats. Never give your pet cheese or junk food such as candy, chocolate, or chips!

Food for Mice

Mice have tiny stomachs. Do not overfeed your pet or it may be overweight. Give mice about a tablespoon of rodent pellets every day. Also feed them treats occasionally. Good treats for mice are a slice of apple, a few blueberries, tiny pieces of carrot, and broccoli. Make sure fruits and vegetables are washed before you give them to your pet. Give your pet fresh water in a drinking bottle every day.

Keeping Healthy

A clean home, fresh water, and the right kind of food will help keep your pet healthy. Check your pet every day for signs of sickness.

Playtime

All pets need something to do to stop them from getting bored and stressed. Give your pet plenty of toys and safe things to chew. Chewing is natural behavior. Play with your pet every day and give it some time to exercise outside its cage or hutch.

Fly Strike

Check your rabbit's rear end every day and clean it if it's dirty. Poop attracts flies, which lay eggs on the rabbit's body. The eggs hatch into maggots, which will burrow into a rabbit's body and make it very sick. If left untreated, fly strike (myiasis) can kill a rabbit. Take your rabbit to the vet if you think it has fly strike.

A Clean Home

It's important for your pet's health to keep its home clean. Take out any soiled bedding, litter, and uneaten fresh food every day. Once a week, be sure to thoroughly clean out the cage and litter box. Use a pet-safe cleaner and rinse everything well. Replace the bedding and nesting material. Never use cedar or pine shavings for bedding. They can make your pet sick. Keep a little of the unsoiled bedding to put back in the cage so it still smells like home!

A Trip to the Vet

Check your pet's teeth and nails regularly. They can grow too long and cause health problems. Take your pet to the vet if its teeth or nails are too long. Rabbits need to be treated for worms, fleas, and ticks. They also need shots to prevent disease. Rats and mice do not need shots. Take them to the vet for a checkup every six months.

Signs Your Pet May Be Sick

❋ Not eating or drinking.

❋ Staying in the nest during times it is usually active.

❋ Scaly patches on the skin.

❋ Runny eyes or nose, sneezing or wheezing.

❋ Diarrhea.

❋ Swellings on the body.

❋ Unsteadiness on the feet or falling over.

Take your pet to the vet if you think it is sick.

In the Wild

Rabbits live in many parts of the world, except southern South America, Asia, and Antarctica. Rats and mice live all over the world apart from Antarctica.

Where Rabbits Live

In the wild, rabbits live in meadows, woods, forests, grasslands, deserts, and wetlands. Cottontail rabbits live in the Americas. Pet rabbits are descended from the European rabbit. It originally came from southwest Europe and northwest Africa. The European rabbit has been introduced to many parts of the world, such as Australia, New Zealand, and South America.

Wild Rats

Wild rats dig and live in underground burrows. A group of females and their young live in a burrow, where they build nest chambers. The burrow may be defended by one male, or there may be several males who share the burrow. Like mice, rats are nocturnal. Although rats and mice are related, they should never be kept in the same enclosure together.

Field Mice

Mice are nocturnal—they are active at night. They do not have very good eyesight, but they have excellent hearing. In the wild, they build long underground burrows where they live. One male usually lives with several females and their young. Pet mice are domesticated forms of the house mouse rather than the field mouse.

Himalayan Rabbit

The Himalayan rabbit is calm, friendly, and intelligent. It is one of the most popular rabbit breeds in the world.

Where in the World?

The Himalayan rabbit probably comes from China, not the Himalayan mountains. It has also been called the Chinese, Russian, and Egyptian rabbit. The breed was taken to England in the mid-1800s and arrived in the United States in the early 1900s.

The Himalayan rabbit is easy to look after.

Pet Care

The Himalayan is a sociable rabbit that likes company. Keep two females, two males, or a neutered male and female together.

❋ Feed your pet good-quality hay and pellets, as well as plenty of fresh leaves and vegetables.

❋ The Himalayan likes playtime—give your pet toys to play with.

Profile

The Himalayan, or Himmie, has a white coat with colored markings on its nose, ears, feet, and tail. These markings can be black, blue, chocolate, or lilac. The markings get darker in cold climates. The Himalayan weighs about 2.5 to 4.5 pounds (1 to 2 kg). It has a long, slender body and red eyes. The Himmie can live for up to 10 years.

Holland Lop Rabbit

The Holland lop is a charming little rabbit with floppy ears. It likes affection and is easy to handle.

Holland lops are intelligent and quiet.

Where in the World?

The first person to breed Holland lops was a Dutchman, Adrian de Cock. He bred Holland lops in the 1950s. Holland lops were brought to the United States in 1976. They were recognized as a breed in the U.S. in 1979.

Pet Care

The Holland lop is intelligent and can be trained to use a litter box. It is playful and active.

❋ Groom your Holland lop every day with a soft brush to keep its fur in good condition.

❋ Feed your pet plenty of good-quality hay and pellets, as well as fresh vegetables.

Profile

The Holland lop has a broad body with a round head and full cheeks. As with all lop rabbits, it has long ears that hang on either side of its head. It comes in a variety of colors, including gray, brown, black, and fawn. It weighs about 3.5 pounds (1.6 kg). The Holland lop lives for about 10 years.

Jersey Wooly Rabbit

The Jersey Wooly was originally bred to be a small pet rabbit.
It has since become very popular as a show rabbit.

Where in the World?

The first person to breed the Jersey Wooly was Bonnie Seeley of New Jersey. She bred French Angoras with Netherlands Dwarfs. She introduced the Jersey Wooly to the American Rabbit Breeders Association in 1984. The Jersey Wooly was recognized as a breed in the United States in 1988.

The Jersey Wooly is a small, gentle rabbit.

Pet Care

Keep Jersey Woolies as house rabbits, rather than keeping them outside. Their small size makes them vulnerable to predators.

❋ The Jersey Wooly's short coat needs grooming about once a week.

❋ It likes lots of attention and playtime. Give it some rabbit-safe toys to play with.

Profile

The Jersey Wooly rabbit has a short, compact body with small, upright ears. It weighs about 3 pounds (1.4 kg). The wooly coat comes in a range of colors, including white, black, chocolate, blue, and tan. The Jersey Wooly lives for about 7 to 10 years.

Standard Rat

The standard rat is a variety of pet rat. It is smaller than a wild rat and has a long body and a thick tail.

Where in the World?

Pet rats are descended from the wild brown, or Norway, rat. Brown rats probably came from China originally. Today, brown rats live in all parts of the world except Antarctica.

The standard rat is the most common type of pet rat.

Pet Care

Pet rats are sociable animals. Keep a pair together to prevent loneliness and boredom.

✱ Give your pet a spacious cage with platforms at different levels and hammocks it can climb into.

✱ Feed your pet good-quality rodent pellets with small pieces of fresh fruits and vegetables.

Profile

Pet rats are smaller than wild rats and have longer tails. The standard rat has a short, smooth, glossy coat. The coat can be one color or patterned. It has long, straight whiskers and round, upright ears. It is about 8 to 10 inches (20 to 25 cm) long from the nose to the base of the tail. Pet rats can live for about two to three years.

Rex Rat

This rat has a curly coat and whiskers. It is a popular pet variety, but always buy from a responsible breeder.

The rex rat comes in a variety of colors.

Where in the World?

Rex rats were first bred in England in 1976. The first rex rats were brought to the United States in 1983.

Pet Care

Like all pet rats, the rex prefers to have the company of at least one other rat in the cage.

✳ Feed your pet good-quality rodent pellets with small pieces of fresh fruits and vegetables.

✳ A rex will start to get bald patches in its coat when it is about 18 months old.

Profile

The rex rat has a curly coat that can be long or short. The curls can be tight or wavy. Rex babies are born with a very curly coat. Males usually have more curls than females. After the first molt at six to seven weeks, the coat loses some of its curl. Rex rats can be one color or a mixture of colors.

Standard Mouse

Pet mice come in many different varieties. The standard mouse has a glossy coat and black or pink eyes.

Where in the World?

Pet mice are descended from the house mouse. Many different types exist today. The house mouse was originally from Europe and Asia north of the Himalayas and North Africa. It has been introduced to many parts of the world, such as the Americas, Australia, and southern Africa.

The standard mouse is the most common kind of pet mouse.

Pet Care

Mice are social animals and are best kept in pairs or groups. Keep two females or two males together or a neutered male and female pair.

✳ Give your pet a spacious cage with different levels for climbing.

✳ Feed your mouse small amounts of rodent pellets, seed mix, and fresh fruits and vegetables.

Profile

Pet mice range from hairless mice to long-haired Angora mice. Standard mice have a short, smooth coat. It can be one color, such as black or white, all over or be a mixture of colors. Pet mice are about 8 to 9 inches (20 to 23 cm) long from nose to tail tip. They usually live for about one to two years.

27

Easy-to-Make
Fun Zone

Make a fun zone for your pet out of cardboard. Put some toys and treats inside, and your pet will love it!

You Will Need:

* Cardboard box(es)
* Scissors
* Newspaper
* Tape
* Paper towel tubes
* Tissues or old phone book

1 Use a box the right size for your pet. A shoe box is perfect for rats and mice. Rabbits need a box big enough for them to move around in.

2 Remove any old tape or staples from the box. Ask an adult to cut doorways and windows in the box.

3 Line the bottom of the box with pieces of cardboard or scrunched-up newspaper. Tape some cardboard pieces to the insides to create "rooms."

4 Put some paper towel tubes in the box for your pet to run through or push around.

5 Add some tissues or an old phone book for your pet to shred.

6 Hide some food treats or chew toys for your pet to find.

You could make a bigger fun zone by taping two or more boxes together.

Fun Facts

Rats and mice have poor vision, but they have very good hearing and an excellent sense of smell.

The American Rabbit Breeders Association (ARBA) recognizes 49 rabbit breeds.

Rats and mice use their tails to balance, communicate, and control their body temperature.

A mouse can squeeze itself through a space the size of a dime.

Rats and mice belong to a large group of animals called rodents. The group includes squirrels, gerbils, beavers, gophers, and porcupines, among others.

The Karni Mata Temple in India is famous for the 25,000 rats that live there. The rats are worshipped in the temple.

Rabbits have large eyes on either side of their head. They can see almost 360 degrees. They have a small blind spot in front of their face.

Rabbits, along with hares and pikas, belong to the group of animals called lagomorphs. Hares are the biggest animals of the group. Pikas are the smallest.

29

Glossary

burrow (1) hole or tunnel in the ground that an animal makes for shelter. (2) to make a hole or tunnel in something.

domesticated living with people.

flea very small biting insect that lives on animals.

hammock type of bed made of fabric that clips to the cage and hangs free.

litter (1) dry material placed in a litter box. (2) group of young animals born at the same time to the same mother.

maggot young form of a fly that looks like a small worm.

molt lose a covering of skin or hair to make way for new growth.

neutered refers to an animal that has had its sex organs removed so it cannot produce young.

nocturnal active at night.

pellet small, hard ball of food for animals.

predator animal that kills other animals for food.

rodent small animal such as a rat or mouse that has sharp front teeth.

shots see vaccination.

tick very small insect that attaches itself to a larger animal and feeds on it.

vaccination treatment with a substance, called a vaccine, to protect against a particular disease.

vulnerable open to attack or injury, easily harmed or injured.

whiskers long, thin hairs that grow near the mouth of some animals.

worm animal that lives in the stomachs of animals and people.

Further Resources

Books

Barder, Gemma. *Be a Rabbit Expert*. New York, NY: Crabtree Publishing, 2024.

Greenwood, Nancy. *Prizewinning Rabbits*. New York, NY: PowerKids Press, 2023.

Rossiter, Brienna. *My Pet Rabbit*. Mendota Heights, MN: Little Blue Readers, 2023.

Websites

10 Facts About Rats!
www.natgeokids.com/uk/discover/animals/general-animals/facts-about-rats/
Discover cool facts about rats with National Geographic Kids.

Rabbit Facts
www.konnecthq.com/rabbit-facts/
Want more cute facts about rabbits? Check out this fun source.

Rabbits and Hares
www.dkfindout.com/us/animals-and-nature/rabbits-and-hares/
Explore the qualities that make rabbits and hares interesting animals!

Publisher's note to parents and teachers: Our editors have reviewed the websites listed here to make sure they're suitable for students. However, websites may change frequently. Please note that students should always be supervised when they access the internet.

Index